DEVOTIONALS FOR PREGNANT WOMEN.

SPIRITUAL NOURISHMENT FOR EXPECTANT MOTHERS.

BY

<u>REBEKAH KASSIM</u>

DEDICATION

I dedicate this book to my darling husband, **Mark B. Kassim**. I am eternally grateful to God for preserving your life. You have become increasingly precious to me with each passing year; every moment we share is a gift to cherish forever. Thank you for your labor of love in fervent, heartfelt prayers and intercessions for me and our children. Your prayers have availed much, and that is why this book could be written. I love you Honey, you are the best!

AND

My five wonderful children: **Enny, Tobi, Ogo, Dotun, and Simi.** You all are my dream come true. I have thoroughly enjoyed raising you; it has been pure joy! Thank you for providing the life classroom for me to learn the lessons in this book. Each of you is an answer to some specific prayer - individually wrapped gifts, yet uniquely blended. You have made your Dad and me very proud parents. Our deepest desire is for you to maximize your potentials and fulfill your God-given destinies. You are blessed and highly favored.

CONTENTS

FOREWORD

🌹

Rebekah and I have been married for eighteen years, after four years of courtship. The memory of our first date in the year 1986 is still very strong on my mind, we sat together at dinner in a small road-side restaurant, and the subject of marriage and child rearing emerged and established itself as the main theme of our conversation. We soon found out that this was one subject area in which we shared similar views from the outset of our relationship.

Rebekah's passion for bearing and raising children is unmistakable. A few weeks before the arrival of our first baby, she decided to leave her teaching job and lavish the expected baby with love and attention. The warmth of her love and affection has permeated every aspect of our family life.

Our marriage is blessed with five wonderful children. While each pregnancy presented a unique excitement and challenge, the faithfulness of God to His promises concerning child bearing remained the same. It has been a wonderful privilege to watch the progressive fulfillment of those promises in the lives of our children every new day that comes by. These were the scriptures that we cleaved unto and declared during the course of each pregnancy.

Rebekah has gracefully articulated in each devotional the unfailing presence of God in all pregnancy situations - pleasant or precarious, and His zeal in aligning all with His good purposes. When I read this book, I felt a deep sense of achievement and could not help declaring to my wife "Your book is a masterpiece!"

Rebekah's commitment to God and our family has made her stand out as a tremendous winner in child bearing. She is a virtuous woman, a loving wife and an affectionate mother for whom I am forever grateful to God.

I encourage every pregnant woman and expectant father to read this book, and receive the ability and confidence to shape the unborn child in goodness and perfection, through the immense power of God's zeal and faithfulness.

Mark B. Kassim

INTRODUCTION

❧

I had my fourth child, Esther Olusoladotun (A Child of New Beginnings), on November 6, 1998. The labor was short and easy. The baby arrived at 1:45a.m. "Is it a girl?" I asked the doctor. "Yes," she replied. I was exhilarated! Not only because of the safe delivery, but also because I had hoped for a baby girl, having had three sons in a row.

She was just as I had imagined, so pink and pretty. I nursed her to sleep and proceeded to take a nap, when things suddenly took a negative turn. I started hemorrhaging! The midwife rushed to get the doctor, who quickly ordered that I be wheeled to the operating theater. On the way to the theater, a voice reminded me about a friend who recently died from hemorrhaging after childbirth. I instantly realized that I had to take a stand against this negative thought, so I quickly replied. "I didn't come here to die; I came to have a baby." It dawned on me that this was spiritual warfare, but the Lord had prepared me ahead of time; therefore, I was not intimidated. While the doctor treated me, I kept my mind alert with the word of God and fired verses from the scriptures back at the enemy. I told the enemy that I would be the one to nurse my baby, and not a nanny. I quoted the scripture from Isaiah 66:12, that says, "For thus says the Lord, 'Behold, I will extend peace to her like a river, and the glory of the Gentiles like a flowing stream; then you shall feed; on her sides shall you be carried and be dandled on her knees.'"

Back at home, Mark, my husband, woke up at about 3:00a.m and called the hospital to find out how the labor was progressing. However, he did not get a satisfactory response, so he came to check on me. On getting to the theater, he was shocked to find me lying in the pool of my own blood! He laid hands on me and declared: "You shall not die, but live, and declare the works of the Lord" (Ps. 118: 17). He then made calls to our pastors and prayer partners to ask for intercession on my behalf. Soon after that, I stopped bleeding.

According to medical statistics, post-partum hemorrhage was the number one killer of women in Nigeria in 1998. But the Lord mercifully intervened in my situation. Like the woman with the issue of blood, I touched the hem of His garment and I was made whole (Mark 5:29), I walked through the valley of the shadow of death, but He was with me; His rod and His staff comforted me (Ps. 23:4).

Eight years later, the Lord added yet another daughter to our family, making us the proud parents of five beautiful children. Nevertheless, three out of the five deliveries were difficult. This book is the overflow from the grateful heart of a woman who was delivered from death over and over again. The Lord impressed it upon my heart to share with other pregnant women the scriptures, and prayers with which He sustained and delivered me through the process of bringing forth our children.

Blessed be the God and Father of our Lord Jesus Christ, the Father of mercies and God of all comfort, who comforts us in all our tribulation, that we may be able to comfort those who are in any trouble, with the comfort with which we ourselves are comforted by God (2 Cor. 1:3-4).

MORE ABOUT MY PREGNANCY HISTORY

Our fifth and youngest child, Mercy-Grace was born here, in the United States. All her siblings were born in Nigeria; so the medical history of my pregnancies was not readily accessible to the medical team at the onset of the pregnancy. I had to recount my previous pregnancy experiences a number of times, to give the doctors an insight into how best to manage my case. This exercise always floods my heart with gratitude to God for His faithfulness and manifold blessings on my life.

Our first son, **Emmanuel Enioluwa** (meaning: Man of God), was born on October 13, 1991. He arrived on his due date, which was a week shy of our first wedding anniversary. The labor was hitch-free and medically uneventful.

Israel Oluwatobiloba (translated God is the Awesome King), came on October 19, 1993, his due date, which happened to be the eve of our third wedding anniversary. The two-hour labor was also medically uneventful.

The third boy, **Joshua Ogo-Oluwa** (The Glory of God), was born on August 4, 1996, two weeks before his due date. Serious complications had developed in the course of the pregnancy. In the thirty-sixth week, I was diagnosed with jaundice due to hemolytic anemia, which means that my blood count was low because my body was breaking down its own cells. This was definitely medically challenging. The doctors had hoped that the baby would arrive closer to the due date (which was August 20, 1996); giving me enough time to recover from my illness, as I did not have enough strength to go through labor. Also, I could not undergo a C-section because I was severely anemic.

It, however, turned out that God had other plans; the baby was born several days earlier than the doctors had wished. God supernaturally manifested His glorious power. The baby was delivered normally without surgery, but by angelic strength, since I was still physically very weak. In the course of the labor, I perceived an angelic hand working in my womb, controlling the contractions such that they were stronger and more effective than the contractions I had experienced in the previous two deliveries. Therefore, the labor lasted about one and a half hours only. Joshua's birth was a very sweet victory!

Esther Olusoladotun, (A Child of New Beginnings), was born at full term on November 6, 1998. The details of this delivery are recorded in the introduction of the book.

On August 31, 2006, we had our second baby girl, **Mercy-Grace Similoluwa,** (Enter into God's Rest), at the Inova Fairfax hospital in Virginia, U.S.A. The pregnancy was a pleasant surprise! Her delivery was a miracle. I had fallen into pre-term labor ten weeks before her due date, because my water broke!! I was rushed to the hospital amidst the blare of sirens, and was admitted and placed on bed rest until the time she was born at thirty weeks of gestation. I had labored for her for a whole week!!! The good news about it all was that the baby had no complications at birth and did not require any kind of support system. She weighed 3.5lbs but was very healthy. We are deeply grateful to God for that. She spent the first month of her young life in the neonatal intensive care unit of the hospital. On September 30, 2006, we were allowed to take our bundle of joy home. Blessed be the name of the Lord for His Mercy and Grace.

DEVOTIONALS
(PART I)

ENCOURAGEMENT FOR THE MOM-TO-BE

The following devotionals are original thoughts and promises I discovered from the Bible as I went through the various stages of childbearing. I have chosen to refer to the unborn child in the female gender, simply for the purpose of easy reading. I confidently testify that I have tested these words and have proved them to be true. I have tasted, and seen that the Lord is good. My heart sings to the God of my salvation:

> 'Tis so sweet to trust in Jesus
> Just to take Him at His word
> Just to rest upon His promise
> Just to know "Thus saith the Lord."

Jesus, Jesus, How I trust Him
How I've proved Him o'er and o'er
Jesus, Jesus, Blessed Jesus
O! For grace to trust Him more.

Louisa M.R. Stead (1850-1917).

1. FRUITFULNESS IS A GIFT

Behold, children are a heritage from the Lord; the fruit of the womb is a reward. Happy is the man who has his quiver full of them (Ps. 127:3 & 5a).

"Every good gift and every perfect gift is from above, and comes down from the Father of lights with whom is no variation, or shadow of turning" (James 1:17). Children are God's gifts to us. They are good and perfect gifts from heaven. In the key verse above, The Bible refers to them as the **fruit** of the womb, or the fruit of our body. The psalmist goes on to say that the man who has many children is happy. Therefore, children bring joy into our lives. To emphasize this point, in the next Psalm, he continues: "Your wife shall be like a fruitful vine in the very heart of your house; your children like olive plants all around your table" (Ps. 128:3).

These scripture verses suggest to me that it is the Lord's good pleasure to bless us with children. I also believe that He wants us to have as many as our hearts desire, since they are to surround our table. Not only is fruitfulness a gift, it is also a command. The Lord God commanded Adam and Eve to "Be fruitful and multiply; fill the earth and subdue it; have dominion over the fish of the sea, over the birds of the air, and over every living thing that moves on earth" (Gen. 1:28).

Fruitfulness, in essence gives us the ability to subdue and dominate our world as we multiply. I want to encourage you that being pregnant is a good thing. It is a God-given privilege. You have been chosen to participate in a creative miracle. God wants you to be fruitful, He wants to increase you, enlarge your coast, broaden your horizon, and extend your area of influence. He loves you and is equally excited about your baby. He is willing to help you all the way. You only have to put your trust in Him. He will see you through.

Father, I thank You for giving me the ability to conceive this child. I appreciate Your good thoughts towards me. I thank You for making me fruitful in the land of the living. Amen.

2. A NEW SONG

"No one shall suffer miscarriage or be barren in your land; I will fulfill the number of your days" (Ex. 23:26).

This is the first pregnancy promise I received from the Lord. Early in our marriage, I was very eager to become a Mom. I was disappointed to discover that I was not pregnant after the first month. So, I went before the Lord and wept bitterly. The Spirit of God spoke to me through the key verse above, I meditated on this promise until I believed it. I knew that I would not be barren, neither would I have miscarriages. That was the beginning of my pregnancy discussions with God. I would still receive many more promises in the course of my five pregnancies.

Afterwards, I began to apply my faith by reading books on pregnancy. I learned about a pregnant woman's diet, and planned my meals accordingly. I had received the word into my spirit, and that revelation was affecting my behavior. Ten weeks later, I had my first symptom; I felt dizzy. We scheduled a visit with our family doctor, who confirmed to us that I was with child. We were ecstatic!

There were several barren women in the Bible, but none remained in the state of barrenness. Ranging from Sarah in the Old Testament to Elizabeth in the New, they all became fruitful; their babies were delayed but not denied. Are you still waiting on the Lord for children? Are you afflicted with secondary infertility? There is nothing that is impossible with our God. Hold fast the confession of your hope without wavering, for He who promised is faithful (Heb. 10:23). He will put a new song on your lips. "He maketh the barren woman to keep house, and to be a joyful mother of children. Praise ye the Lord" (Ps. 113:12 KJV).

Father Lord, I thank You because with You, there is no respect of persons. If You could break the yoke of barrenness from all these women in the Bible, You can do it for me and my loved ones too. I receive my children in due season and in rapid succession. Amen.

3. A BIRTH ANNOUNCEMENT

And the angel of the Lord appeared to the woman and said to her, "Indeed now, you are barren and have borne no children, but you shall conceive and bear a son" (Judg. 13:3).

A birth announcement comes to congratulate you for a child that is yet to be conceived. Our key verse is one of such announcements made to Manoah's wife, the mother of Samson. Most of the pregnancies recorded in the Bible were preceded by birth announcements. Angelic messengers were dispatched specially to inform the prospective parents about the baby that was to be born. Sarah, Zechariah, and Mary the mother of Jesus were all privileged and chosen for these angelic visitations.

The common factor in all these stories is that all the women had been barren, while Mary was a virgin. Secondly, all the babies in question had special assignments and a great work to do for God. I believe God did this to activate the faith of the parents, who had probably given up hope of having children, so that they could believe Him for the impossible. Furthermore, a birth announcement gives the parents a preview of the child's purpose in life, thus helping them to raise the child in the fear of the Lord.

Sisters, you might be dealing with an impossible situation with regards to child bearing, the doctors might have told you that you cannot have children, maybe your fallopian tubes are blocked, or you've had a hysterectomy. If these conditions apply, then you qualify for a birth announcement. Allow me to give you this message from the heart of your Father in heaven: **"You will soon be with Child**." The fact that you are holding this book is a sign that the Lord has heard your cry.... "Blessed is she who believed, for there will be a fulfillment of those things which were told her from the Lord" (Luke 1:45).

Dear Lord, I believe Your word, may it prosper in my life. Make me a fruitful vine around my husband's house; let my children surround my table like olive plants. Amen.

4. FEARFULLY AND WONDERFULLY MADE

For You formed my inward parts; You covered me in my mother's womb. I will praise You, for I am fearfully and wonderfully made: Marvelous are your works, and that my soul knows very well. (Ps. 139:13-14).

The Bible records that God created the Earth in seven days. From the first day to the fifth, the Lord spoke everything He created into being. ' "Let there be light': and there was light"(Gen. 1:3)...and so on, but on the sixth day, "The Lord God formed man of the dust of the ground, and breathed into his nostrils the breath of life; and man became a living soul (Gen. 2:7). God did not speak man into existence; He made man after His own image. God still makes human beings; the only difference is that He makes them in our wombs.

Immediately after conception, your uterus becomes God's workshop as it were. In the coming days, He will be fashioning the delicate parts of your offspring in the darkness of your womb. Your baby is God's handiwork: "As you do not know what is the way of the wind, **or how the bones grow in the womb of her that is with child**; so you do not know the works of God who makes everything" (Eccl. 11:5). Furthermore, the Bible says "**Before I formed you in the womb, I knew you; before you were**

born, I sanctified you, and I ordained you a prophet to the nations" (Jer. 1:5).

From the above listed scriptures, we realize that God knew the baby prior to conception, formed her while in the womb. He then sets her apart for a specific purpose, before she is born. Rejoice, because your child is a masterpiece, she is blessed, she is chosen, and she is fearfully and wonderfully made.

Dear Lord, I thank You for the great work You are doing in my body. I pray that my baby will be filled with Your Spirit and sanctified unto You. Amen.

5. NOURISHED BY THE LIVING WATERS

He shall be like a tree planted by the rivers of water, that brings forth its fruit in its season, whose leaf also shall not wither; and whatsoever he does shall prosper (Ps. 1:3).

Psalm One is popularly known as the Psalm of the Righteous Man. Who would have thought that it is also for pregnant women? Well, if you are pregnant and righteous (Jesus Christ has made you righteous by His blood), then this Psalm is for you. There are three promises hidden in this favorite scripture:

The first one is that you are "Like a tree planted by the streams of water." The Bible says "Out of your belly shall flow rivers of living water" (John 7:38), via the Holy Spirit who dwells in you. The child in your belly is actually situated very close to the source of this water. As your body provides physical nutrition to the fetus, the Spirit of God inside of you supplies the spiritual nutrition your baby needs. A tree that is planted by the rivers flourishes, even in the time of famine when other trees are fruitless; this tree brings forth its fruit in its season. Therefore you shall bring forth your baby in due season, at the right and perfect time.

Secondly: "Your leaves also shall not wither." When leaves wither off of a tree, it is a sign of ill-health or even death of the tree due to malnutrition. But because you are being nourished by the Spirit of

31

God, you will be healthy throughout your pregnancy. There shall be no miscarriage or loss of life. You will live and your baby will live.

The final promise says, "Whatsoever you do shall prosper." This promise goes for the totality of your being: your pregnancy, health, marriage, job, and other interpersonal relationships. Prosperity in every area of your life ensures a positive and pleasant pregnancy. It makes the temporary discomforts of gestation bearable, and also makes the baby's arrival more exciting. *Bon voyage!*

Dear Lord Jesus, You are the word of life. As I meditate on Your word, let it bring nourishment to me; and to the baby in my womb. Amen.

6. MARY TOO?

And Mary remained with her about three months, and returned to her house (Luke 1:56).

I had heard different stories of early pregnancy experiences; however, I found myself absolutely unprepared for the dizziness, morning sickness and evening weakness that heralded the conception of our offspring. The first trimester stretched on and on like an eternity. Although, I was very excited about the pregnancy, I was wondering why I had to be so sick! As I studied the word and prayed, the Spirit of God comforted me with this key verse above. Why did Mary spend the first trimester of her pregnancy in Elizabeth's house?

Mary had learned from the angel Gabriel that her elderly cousin was experiencing a miracle pregnancy. She probably went to confirm the angel's report and to rejoice with Elizabeth. She also needed to share her good news with someone who could believe her story. Having said that, I could not help but wonder... was Mary dealing with morning sickness...was she tired and short of breath...was she on compulsory bed rest ...like me? Maybe she was.

Mary probably spent the bulk of her time meditating on the Old Testament, the Spirit of God revealing to her prophecies concerning her baby. She had a lot to learn...to understand ...and so much to hide in her heart about this GOD-MAN in her womb.

So do you Sisters. This is your time to meditate on the word of God. It is time to worship and sing praises unto the Lord. It is time to have a heart-to-heart communion with your Maker...and the Maker of your baby.

Dear Lord, I rest my heart at Your feet; as I study your word, let it bring life unto my flesh and strength to my womb. Amen.

7. WHOSE REPORT WILL YOU BELIEVE?

Praise the Lord, O Jerusalem; praise your God, O Zion. For He has strengthened the bars of your gates; He has blessed your children within you (Ps. 147:12-13).

Because of the severity of my sickness and some other symptoms I experienced in the early weeks of my first pregnancy, the doctors feared that I might lose the baby through **'spontaneous abortion'** so I was placed on bed rest. Whose report would I believe? I chose to believe the report of the Lord which said that I would not suffer miscarriage. Fortunately, the bed rest worked in my favor, because I had long uninterrupted times to seek God's face and meditate on His word. Anytime the enemy sowed a seed of fear in my mind, God always gave me a specific scripture to destroy fear and put faith in its place.

That was how I received this pregnancy promise. God told me to praise him because He had strengthened the bars of my gates. Which gates? The gates of my uterus: or my **cervix**. He said to me that He had kept the embryo safe within my womb by strengthening my cervix. Therefore, it became impossible for me to cast my young through spontaneous abortion. Moreover, He promised me that He had blessed all my children within me; referring to the baby I was then expecting, and my other children that were yet to be born. I am able to write this book, because God kept His word.

I don't know what, if any, negative report a doctor may have given you about your pregnancy. Whose report will you believe? Choose to believe the report of the Lord. Stand on the wonderful promises of God. The report of the Lord is that you will not have a miscarriage. Your child is safe and secure. She is blessed within you. As you believe and boldly confess the word, the Lord will turn any negative situation around for your good. "For with God, nothing will be impossible" (Luke 1:37).

Dear Father, I thank You that nothing will happen to me during this pregnancy that You and I cannot handle. Help me to believe Your report above all else. Amen.

8. A PREGNANCY JUST NOW?

And the angel of the Lord said to her: "Behold, you are with child, and you shall bear a son, Ishmael, because the Lord has heard your affliction" (Gen. 16:11).

Sarah, the beloved but barren wife of Abraham, had a bright idea. She advised her husband to go in unto her maid, Hagar. Her plan was for Hagar to be the surrogate mother for her children. The plan turned sour when Hagar got pregnant and despised her mistress. So, Sarah dealt harshly with Hagar until she could take it no more. Hagar fled!

Has an unplanned pregnancy shown up in your womb? Maybe you are a teenager, or you are on your way back to school. You may want to start a business and not a family. You might have many children already and cannot afford another mouth to feed. Is this pregnancy a result of sexual molestation? An unexpected pregnancy...this is a rather hard place to be.

It is women at these cross-roads who are most tempted to abort their babies. A pregnancy devotional cannot be complete without the mention of abortion. It is a very present evil in our world. The enemy will tempt you sorely to terminate the pregnancy; after all, "Is it not just a blob of tissue?" Sisters, do not believe the lie. Abortion is an abomination in God's sight; it steals your promise and leaves you with an empty womb and a broken heart. "Therefore **choose**

life; that both you and your descendants may live" (Deut. 30:19b).

How did Hagar get out of this predicament? The Lord God saw Hagar in the wilderness as she fled from Sarah. He sent an angel to encourage and bless her and the child in her womb. God has seen you beloved. He has heard your affliction. He knows exactly where you are at. Surely His angels are on assignment to minister to you, for you and your offspring are heirs of salvation (Heb. 1:14).

Dear Lord Jesus, help me. I need Your grace and wisdom. Strengthen me by Your Spirit in my inner person. Make all things about this pregnancy to work together for my good. Amen.

9. MARY, DID YOU KNOW?

He will be great, and will be called the Son of the Highest: and the Lord God will give him the throne of His father David (Luke 1:32).

I love the words of the famous Christmas carol. **"Mary, did you know?"** by Mark Lowry and Buddy Greene.

Mary did you know that your Baby boy would
    someday walk on water?
Mary did you know that your Baby boy would
    save our sons and daughters?
Did you know that your Baby boy has come
    to make you new?
This child that you delivered will soon deliver
    you.

Mary did you know that your Baby boy will
    give sight to a blind man?
Mary did you know that your Baby boy will
    calm the storm with His hand?
Did you know that your Baby boy has walked
    where angels trod?
When you kissed your little Baby, you kissed
    the face of God?

Although, Mary had an idea about Jesus' mission on Earth, she could not have imagined the magnitude of the miracles that Jesus would perform. She probably did not know that Jesus would be crucified and be raised from the dead. Neither did she perceive, when she kissed her little baby, that she kissed the face of God.

Mom-to-be, who is the baby in your womb? Is he like Moses the great deliverer, Abraham Lincoln, or Albert Einstein? Is she like Deborah, the mother in Israel, Mother Theresa, or Princess Diana? Did the mothers of these great people know who their children were, or what they would become? They probably didn't.

What distinguishes the pregnancy of a great man or woman from others? I believe every pregnancy follows the natural pattern, therefore, treat your unborn child with utmost care and respect. You might be expecting the next Billy Graham, or the next Nelson Mandela. Who knows? You just might be the chosen Mom of the person that will shape the history of the 21st century.

Dear Father, thank You for the great plans You have for my baby; help me to raise her in Your admonition. Teach me to lead her in the path of her destiny. Amen.

10. A CHILD OF NEW BEGINNINGS

Then David comforted Bath-sheba his wife, and went in to her and lay with her. So she bore a son, and he called his name Solomon. Now the Lord loved him (2 Sam. 12:24).

Some babies are conceived after a family tragedy, such as a recent miscarriage, or the death of a child. David and Bathsheba sinned before the Lord by committing adultery. Although they repented, they still lost their first child. Then King David comforted Bathsheba in love. The Lord blessed her and she conceived Solomon, whom the Lord chose above all of David's sons to reign in his stead.

Also, a family may go through a season of trials and tribulations. God may use the conception of a baby to herald the end of that season and the beginning of a new one. My fourth child was conceived after my family had just come out of difficult times. My husband had been sick with a life-threatening disease, but after much prayers and supplications, the Lord healed him. Shortly after that, I discovered I was pregnant again! The pregnancy was a pleasant and comforting surprise. So, we called the child **"Olusoladotun,"** which means "The Lord Has Given Me a New Beginning."

Someone reading this book may be in a similar situation. Maybe you had a miscarriage, or recently lost a child. You might be going through different kinds of affliction. Be encouraged. The good Lord will comfort you in the innermost parts of your being. He will heal your wounds, and give you a new beginning. "Remember ye not the former things, neither consider the things of old. 'Behold, I will do a new thing; now it shall spring forth: shall you not know it? I will even make a road in the wilderness and rivers in the desert' " (Isa. 43:18-19).

Dear Father of mercies and God of all comfort, I receive the comfort of Your Spirit in my heart. I thank You for giving me a new beginning. Amen.

11. WHAT IS THE BABY'S NAME? (I)

*The Lord has called me from the womb; from
the matrix of my mother He has made mention
of my name (Isa. 49:1b).*

I love to ask parents for the names of their children. I probe further for the meaning of the name
and their reason for choosing it. Most parents tell
me that God gave them the specific name for their
own child. In the Bible days, children were named
by their mothers. In some special situations like that
of the Lord Jesus Christ and His forerunner, John the
Baptist, the names were revealed by angels.

It is the privilege and responsibility of the parents
to seek God's face for the name that God gave the
baby while she was in the womb. This is important
because the child's name affects her personality. The
God-given name also reveals the child's purpose and
destiny. "And you shall call His name JESUS; for He
will save His people from their sins" (Matt. 1:21).
In the case of John the Baptist, the family members
were surprised that he was not named after Zechariah.
God gave John a different name, because his calling
and purpose in life was different from his father's.
Zechariah was a priest, while John was a prophet.

The Lord, in His sovereignty, may also choose
to reveal the child's name to grandparents or some
extended family member. As you pray, the Holy
Spirit may send the answer to a close family friend,
especially if they have been interceding for you. In

such a situation, there will be a witness with your spirit that the name is from God. Naming our children was an important part of all my five pregnancies. We received their names by direct revelation, through circumstances, or by prophecy. It has been such a joy to watch them live up to their God-given identities!

Father Lord, all the families in heaven and earth are named in You. As we seek Your face, reveal to us the name on Your mind for this child in my womb. Let Your name be glorified in her life. Amen.

12. WHAT IS THE BABY'S NAME? (II)

And Jabez was more honorable than his brethren: and his mother called him Jabez, saying, "Because I bare him with sorrow" (1 Chron. 4:9 KJV).

Pregnancies come with various challenges; however, some can be called difficult. A pregnancy may keep you on bed rest for several weeks, or have you visiting the emergency room for nine months. Some pregnancies may be progressing with relative normalcy, until there is a sudden change in the mother's circumstances – loss of a loved one, financial stress, political unrest, economic instability, war, or famine.

Everything about the pregnancy and delivery of Israel, my second son, was perfect (I thank God for that). However, I was stressed by external factors. There was a major political crisis in Nigeria at the time. It was the worst we had had since the civil war, and it dragged for many months. So, I was restless in my spirit. I spent most of my time during this pregnancy praying for the nation, both individually, in my closet, and corporately, with other believers. The national problem was miraculously resolved just before I gave birth to him.

We were not told the type of difficulty Jabez's Mom had when she gave birth to him. However, she thought the problem was so bad that she associated his name with "**Sorrow.**" She missed it. The name limited his possibilities and marked him for disasters. Jabez prayed to God for a name change and God heard him. He gave him a new identity: "**Honorable.**" This shows us that God is not in the business of giving His children negative names. Whatever you may be going through; put your trust in God. He will change your situation through your baby's name.

Dear Lord, I humbly bow my heart before You in adoration and worship. I trust that Your great plan for my baby still stands; my present situation not withstanding. Choose a name for my baby that will glorify you. Amen.

DEVOTIONALS
(PART II)

PRAYERS FOR THE BABY

🌹

This book is primarily written for the expectant mother. However, I am including a couple of devotionals on praying for the baby in the womb. This is to inspire and encourage you to pray for your baby as soon as the pregnancy is confirmed. In addition to praying God's word for your child, you also want to pray specifically about your aspirations and dreams for her as the Holy Spirit leads you.

I would like to give my husband the credit for these prayers. He would faithfully lay hands on my growing belly every night for nine months. He would pray all manner of prayers, both in the Spirit and in the understanding. Seeing the positive effects of these prayers on Emmanuel, our first son, encouraged us to repeat the process during the subsequent pregnancies. The following devotionals contain our favorite prayers for our children when they were in the womb.

13. THE BABY'S EMOTIONS IN THE WOMB

For indeed; as soon as the voice of your greeting sounded in my ears, the babe leaped in my womb for joy (Luke 1:44).

In this key verse, the Bible gives us an insight into what goes on in the darkness of a pregnant woman's womb. Elisabeth heard the sound of Mary's voice, but John in her womb heard the voice of Jesus through Mary's salutation, He leapt for joy.

From this story we can conclude that babies have emotions even while in the womb. If a baby could be happy in the womb, it also means that the opposite is true; they could be sad, or anxious. Naturally, we desired for our children to be happy, so we started praying for them as soon as they were conceived. We prayed that the totality of their time in the womb would be a joyful experience for them and that they would be calm and filled with the peace of God that passes all understanding. Medical research has shown that a child in the womb can pick up her mother's prevailing emotions. So, in addition to praying, be happy. You need to really want the baby. Even if you are feeling sick and tired, you can still be positive and joyful in pregnancy.

The mother's environment is equally important. The text above says that John rejoiced at the sound of Mary's voice because he recognized the presence of the Lord. May I suggest that you keep your baby around Jesus? Go to church as regularly as you can. Do not neglect the fellowship of other believers. (Heb. 10:25) Let your child get used to the presence of the Holy Spirit in your home. Fill your life with His praises. Your child will hear His voice and she will leap for joy!

Sweet Holy Spirit, I pray that You fill me till my cup overflows. Fill my baby with Your presence even in the womb. Let her have fellowship with You. Amen.

14. THE BABY'S NEEDS

He brought them forth also with silver and gold: and there was not one feeble person among their tribes (Ps. 105:37 KJV).

This text refers to the time God delivered the Israelites from Egypt. Surely, the Lord brought them out with silver and gold. He told them to borrow jewelry from the Egyptians, and by doing so, the Israelites came out of slavery a rich nation. We started praying with this verse as far back as the pregnancy of our first son. This was because we discovered that the baby's paraphernalia was going to cost us some money.

The Lord had graciously taught us to depend on Him for supplies early in our marriage. We continued to trust Him as we made room for this all-important addition to the family. We prayed this verse every night. "Lord, let our son be brought forth with silver and gold." In other words, we prayed that he would be born with a silver spoon in his mouth.

There are lots of needs to be met at the arrival of a baby, both medical and material. There are needs for the new Mom, and sometimes, need for a baby sitter or childcare services. The list is endless. Having a baby will task your finances, but cheer up, for our God is able. He gave you the baby. He can supply her needs. Pray ahead for the needs to be met. Pray that silver and gold will come as your child is brought forth. God did it for us. He will do it for you too.

"But my God shall supply all your need according to His riches in glory by Christ Jesus" (Phil. 4:19). Amen.

Dear Father, I thank You for Your willingness to provide for my baby. I put my trust in You and I know that my child will not lack any good thing. May all her needs be supernaturally supplied according to Your riches in glory. Amen.

15. THE BABY'S HEALTH

He brought them forth also with silver and gold: and there was not one feeble person among their tribes (Ps. 105:37 KJV).

It is estimated that about three million Israelites left Egypt on foot. In the previous devotional, we saw how God enriched them. Additionally, this scripture records that there was not one sick person among the twelve tribes. That was a miracle! The same God who did that has not changed. He can do it again.

Health problems in the unborn child are a major concern for expectant parents. The Lord has promised not to put any of the diseases of the Egyptians on us. So, stand your ground against any kind of weakness in your baby. This is Mark's favorite verse. We prayed every night for our children, as they were being formed in the womb, that they would be strong and healthy; that their genes would be good; and that there would be no sickness in any of their organs. All our children were born healthy. Even when I had difficult deliveries, the babies were perfect. We did not take this for granted. We know that God answered our prayers.

"There was none feeble among their **tribes:**" This means nobody was sick in that generation. Beloved, you and your children constitute a tribe. If there has been a generational sickness in your lineage, pray that the errant chromosome be removed from your children's genes. Claim this promise for the child in the womb, and all the other children in your tribe, including those yet to be conceived. God will turn every negative situation around. He is willing and well able to give you hale and hearty babies.

Father God, I bless Your name today, I thank You for Your promise to give me a healthy baby. I believe Your word and receive my baby in perfect health. Amen.

DEVOTIONALS (PART III)

FAMOUS BIBLE PREGNANCIES

I am glad that the Bible is so comprehensive. There is nothing that we might be going through that God has not documented for us in His word. Although we have referred to many pregnancies in the Bible, I would like to take a closer look at the famous ones. These pregnancies got special mention because they were miraculous; yet each of them is unique. Here are some nuggets of wisdom to refresh and enlighten us further in our meditations and devotions.

16. SARAH'S FAITH

Through faith also Sarah herself received strength to conceive seed, and was delivered of a child when she was past age, because she judged him faithful who had promised (Heb. 11: 11).

Sarah's pregnancy was truly miraculous; not only had she passed child-bearing age, she was also very old. Prior to that time, it had not happened that a woman conceived a child after menopause. Her case looked hopeless. Little did she know that God was preparing her for an unprecedented miracle. Definitely, the Lord renewed every cell in her body to make her womb ready to receive seed and nurture the fetus.

In the key verse above, we see that Sarah had gotten pregnant by faith. The Bible is very vocal about Abraham's faith, but in this text, it sheds more light on Sarah's relationship with God. She was a woman of faith in her own right. Although she laughed when the angel gave the birth announcement, she believed the promise. It was her faith that gave her the strength to conceive seed and carry the pregnancy to full term.

How does this relate to us? Many of us reading this book are definitely younger than ninety years old. We are probably in the prime of our lives, but wherever we are on the journey; a woman still needs faith to conceive. The Bible says also that she needed faith for delivery of the baby. Even though you may not have needed faith for conception, you still need faith for the D-day. Maybe you are past thirty-five years and the doctor says your pregnancy is high risk? Be a daughter of Sarah. Put your faith to work.

Dear Father, I thank You for giving me the strength to conceive this child. By Your grace, I will carry this pregnancy to term. Let my faith in You continue to grow. Amen.

17. ISAAC PRAYED.

Now Isaac pleaded with God for his wife, because she was barren; and the Lord granted his plea, and Rebekah his wife conceived (Gen. 25:21).

Isaac and Rebekah were very close in their marital relationship. Theirs was the dream marriage, perfectly ordained by God. However, Rebekah was barren for twenty years! Isaac must have felt real compassion for her. He pled with God for his wife with a deep burden that could only have come from a loving husband. He prayed for her in his capacity as the priest of his home. The Lord heard him and his wife became pregnant. It was Isaac's prayers that broke the curse of barrenness on Rebekah's life.

A book for pregnant women cannot be complete without the mention of the expectant father, **your husband**. I am blessed by a husband who prayed for me throughout all of my pregnancies. It was relatively easy for me to conceive (I had two oops babies!), but I really needed prayers in labor. Mark's heartfelt and timely prayers availed much for me when I had difficult deliveries.

The role of a husband in the life of a pregnant woman cannot be over-emphasized. If you, like Rebekah, are still waiting on the Lord for children; humbly ask for your husband's prayers. If you are pregnant already; let your husband know exactly the challenges you are facing, so that he can pray for you accurately. Let him lay his hands on your belly and pray for the baby in your womb. If you are single and pregnant; or pregnant, but your spouse is not available, get all the prayer support you can from your close friends and your church's intercessory group. "Again I say to you that if two of you agree on earth concerning anything that they ask, it will be done for them by my father in heaven" (Matt. 18:19).

Dear Lord Jesus, I thank You for the blessing of a loving and praying spouse. Thank You for filling my life with wonderful friends and family. May their prayers avail for me and may I be faithful to pray for my pregnant friends. Amen.

18. REBEKAH INQUIRED OF THE LORD

But the children struggled together within her; and she said, "If all is well, why am I like this?" So she went to inquire of the Lord (Gen. 25: 22).

Rebekah was having a rather difficult time with this pregnancy. She had heard many pregnancy stories, but no one seemed to have any explanation for her situation. The Lord had compensated her doubly for the barrenness she had earlier endured. She had conceived twins! She was the first woman in the Bible to be conferred with such an honor. Meanwhile, the two babies wrestled inside her. Surely, that did not feel like a normal pregnancy. It definitely wasn't. So what did she do? She went to inquire of the Lord.

The Lord gave her the first sonogram ever. She got to know what was happening in the darkness of her womb. She was going to have two children at once! Rebekah was also privileged to catch a glimpse of her children's future. She must have left the place of inquiry with awe. She was definitely ecstatic at the news of twins...she also had some secrets to hide in her heart about the two nations that struggled within her.

Rebekah's story should encourage the modern-day Christian woman to dialogue with God about her baby. The Bible says; "Call to Me, and I will answer you and show you great and mighty things which you do not know" (Jer. 33:3).There is no telling what God may reveal to you, if you seek His face concerning this pregnancy. Why ask? Asking about your baby and receiving the answer gives you the confidence that God is with you on this journey. Oh! What blessed assurance!

Dear Lord Jesus, draw me close to You. May I feel so comfortable in Your presence that I am able to pour out my needs and challenges to You even before I talk to the doctors. Open the eyes of my heart that I might behold great and mighty things in righteousness. Amen.

19. MANOAH'S WIFE: A SPECIAL DIET.

"Now therefore, please be careful not to drink wine or similar drink and not to eat anything unclean" (Judg. 13: 4).

The Bible did not tell us the name of Samson's mother. She was simply introduced as Manoah's barren wife. She gets a birth announcement from an angel. This announcement was unique in that it came with some dietary restrictions. The child was a **Nazarite**. He had been separated unto God from the womb, so the mother must not drink wine. Neither could she eat any unclean food. Manoah's wife obeyed the instructions fully. That was why Samson could fulfill his purpose.

I remember filling out forms at the Women and Children's Hospital in Los Angeles County, California, when I was expecting Mercy-Grace, our fifth child. There were three recurrent questions on the forms: "Do you drink?" "Do you smoke?" "Are you on drugs?" These questions echo the angel's restriction diet for Manoah's wife. It is an established fact that women who drink and smoke give birth to babies with low birth weight, while women on drugs run the risk of having deformed babies. Drinking and smoking diminish the womb's capacity to sustain life.

Get a couple of good pregnancy health books and learn about pregnancy diets. In addition to eating right, it is important to get enough rest and proper exercise. If you are struggling with drinking, smoking, or drugs; seek professional help. Pray that God will deliver you from every form of addiction. The Lord will gloriously set you free, so you and your children will be free indeed (John 8:36).

Dear Lord Jesus, I thank You for dying for me. My body is Your temple; help me to keep my temple pure and holy in Your sight. Grant me the wisdom and the self control to eat right so that my womb will yield healthy babies. Amen.

20. ELISABETH'S PROPHETIC PREGNANCY.

And Elizabeth was filled with the Holy Spirit; then she spoke out with a loud voice and said "Blessed are you among women, and blessed is the fruit of your womb" (Luke 1: 41b-42).

The peculiar fact about Elisabeth's pregnancy was that this time around, the birth announcement goes to the father, Zechariah. The couple feared and loved the Lord, but they were just too old to have a child...were they really? Zechariah reacted skeptically to the angel Gabriel's glad tidings. As a sign, Zechariah was rendered unable to speak until after his foretold son, John, was born.

Elisabeth got pregnant indeed as the Lord had spoken. The Lord had done exceedingly more than she could ask or think. The Lord looked on her and removed her reproach among people. Afterwards, a pregnant Mary visited Elisabeth. John's leap for joy in his mother's womb activated the anointing of the Holy Ghost on her, and she prophesied mysteries unto Mary about the Child Jesus, as recorded in the key verse above.

What might your pregnancy be saying? Could God be using your state of pregnancy as a source of hope for mothers-in-waiting? He may choose to use your pregnancy to reveal himself to some family member. Your pregnancy may start a season of fruitfulness in your extended family. God may use your pregnancy as a sign of new beginnings and times of refreshing. You may be getting a name-change with this pregnancy. Discern by the Holy Spirit what the Lord wants to achieve through your pregnancy. Be a willing vessel. Yield yourself to Him. He will speak mysteries through your life. "Here am I and the children whom the Lord has given me! We are for signs and wonders in Israel from the Lord of hosts, who dwells in mount Zion" (Isa. 8:18).

Dear Lord Jesus, use me. I am your handmaiden; I yield my life to You. Make me a witness of Your goodness and Your glory in this generation. Amen.

21. MARY BLESSED THE LORD.

And Mary said, my soul doth magnify the Lord, and my spirit hath rejoiced in God my Savior (Luke 1: 46-47).

Mary's pregnancy was the most miraculous of all. All the other pregnancies pointed to hers. The Lord God had graciously revealed His mighty power in the preceding pregnancies, so that we could believe in the virgin birth of Jesus Christ. I always marvel at Mary's quiet but solid confidence in God. She also got a birth announcement. She did not argue with the angel. She embraced her destiny by fully submitting herself to God's plan for her life.

Remember Mary was an unmarried teenager. She literally risked her life by her consent to bear the Son of God. Joseph could have left her, but she trusted that God would take care of her. And He did. Therefore, she blessed God and rejoiced in her spirit. She was thrilled that God would even consider using her for such a great assignment. God had not chosen someone mighty or rich. He had chosen one of the meek and the lowly. She recognized what an honor that was, because from then on every generation would call her **"Blessed."** That prospect was enough for her. She humbly yielded herself as a vessel to give us the greatest gift ever: **JESUS CHRIST.**

The gift Mary gave to us 2000 years ago continues to give. She had given the world a gift that could not die. Jesus Christ, the Son of God was born that we might be redeemed. He died for our sins and transgressions. He rose up on the third day for our justification. Perhaps, you are reading this book and are yet to give your life to the Lord Jesus Christ. Would you consider doing so now? Ask Him to come into your heart by faith. The Bible says that, "If you confess with your mouth the Lord Jesus, and believe in your heart that God hath raised Him from the dead, you will be saved" (Rom. 10:9).

Lord Jesus, I am a sinner. I believe that You died for me and that You rose up on the third day for my redemption. I give my life to You today. I accept You as my Lord and Savior. Use me Lord, for Your glory. Amen.

DEVOTIONALS (PART IV)

DEVOTIONS FOR DELIVERY

A woman, when she is in travail hath sorrow because her hour is come: but as soon as she is delivered of the child, she remembereth no more the anguish for joy that a man is born into the world (John 16:21 KJV).

The delivery of the baby is the end point of pregnancy. The tiny little seed that was planted in the womb nine months ago has come full cycle. It is now due season for you to bring forth your fruit.

There are myriads of promises for delivery in the Bible. The Bible refers to the birth of a child as travail or labor which depicts hard work. The good news is that God is very willing to give us smooth, easy and happy deliveries. In this final series of devotionals, we will examine a few of these precious promises.

22. THE HEBREW WOMEN

And the midwives said to Pharaoh, "Because the Hebrew women are not as the Egyptian women; for they are lively and give birth before the midwives come to them" (Ex. 1:19).

The Egyptian midwives had been given a mandate to kill every Hebrew son at birth, but the fear of the Lord gripped them and they did not. In the key verse above, they presented a reason to Pharaoh for saving the Hebrew baby boys alive, saying that Hebrew women were stronger than Egyptian women.

There was an undeniable grace on the Hebrew women in labor that was not on their Egyptian counterparts. The Lord shortened the duration of their travail, so they brought forth their children before the estimated time. God showed up in the delivery rooms of the Hebrew women. The hand of God on these ladies witnessed to the Egyptian midwives that truly, there was a God in Israel. So they feared God and saved a generation of Hebrew sons. Then God blessed the midwives in return.

I remember that I had absolutely painless contractions as I travailed for our fourth child, Esther. I had gone to the hospital for my regular pre-natal clinic. The midwife examined me and asked "Mrs. Kassim, are you in pain?" I replied, "No, I'm not." Then she said that my cervix was four centimeters dilated and that she could feel my baby's head. I was already in labor, but I was not in pain! The medical team could not understand how that happened. They talked about me all day, declaring that I was a Hebrew woman. I realized that the Lord touched their hearts through this miracle of childbirth. Why does God make delivery easier on His children? He wants us to be His witnesses wherever we go, even in the delivery room. When the world sees His saving grace upon us, they will praise the name of our Father in heaven.

Father, I praise You because Your grace is sufficient for me. As I travail for this child, let Your grace for easy delivery be released upon me. Make my baby's birth a testimony of Your loving kindness. Amen.

23. URGENT PRAYERS OF
A WOMAN IN TRAVAIL

Make haste, O God, to deliver me! Make haste to help me O Lord! But I am poor and needy; make haste to me, O God! You are my help and my deliverer, O Lord, do not delay (Ps. 70:1 & 5).

In the Third World countries, epidurals are not administered to women in labor. I had four out of my five children in Nigeria and had to go through the travails in full force as they are recorded in the Bible. With my first baby, I was somewhat apprehensive of the labor process. This was normal, since I did not know what to expect. I had to depend on God to help me on the day of delivery. Through prayers and meditations in the Word, the Lord encouraged my spirit. By the time the baby was due, I was confident that I could handle the labor pains.

I came across Psalm Seventy in the course of my devotions. I memorized the Psalm, taking the word "**deliver**" in the key verses above, literally as in childbirth. In the early stages of labor, when contractions were few and far between, I would read my Bible. This fascinated the midwives; they joked and said to me, "You are not yet in labor." I quickly understood what they meant, when the long and hard contractions started. I dropped the Bible and started quoting the verses I had memorized. I punctuated every contraction with shouts of "O Lord, deliver me quick!" The Lord heard my cry and delivered me right on time.

Some women have been known to say negative things in labor. This should not be the case with the daughters of the King. Rather, you should saturate your mind with the word of God, then it will spring out from your inner person when you experience pain that is stronger than your brain can process. The spoken word of God will permeate the atmosphere in the delivery room. It will cause all things - the labor pains, the epidural, the midwives and the doctors, to work together for your good. (Rom. 8:28). "Let the word of Christ dwell in you richly in all wisdom; teaching and admonishing one another in psalms and hymns and spiritual songs, singing with grace in your hearts to the Lord" (Col. 3:16).

Dear Lord, I thank you for your Holy Spirit who lives inside of me. As I bring forth this child, let Your praises flow out of my spirit. You are My Lord and my King. I love you Lord. Amen.

24. STRENGTH TO LABOR

That our garners may be full affording all manner of store; that our sheep may bring forth thousands and ten thousands in our street; that our oxen may be strong to labor (Ps. 144:13-14b KJV).

King David was praying for Israel as a king who loved his people and also as one who used to be a shepherd. His expertise with animals is reflected in these key verses. Here, he prayed for the proliferation of Israel's livestock, a vital part of the nation's economy. He prayed that the animals will be **"Strong to labor,"** because he knew that weak animals could not yield many offspring. He understood the importance of the maternal strength of his cattle if they were to have a yield in the thousands and tens of thousands.

If a king could pray for the strength of his flock, how much more should husbands and doctors pray that their wives or patients are strong during labor, bringing forth healthy children? I wonder what it would be like, if every pregnant woman had someone interceding for her as she travails. I believe we would have far fewer stillbirths, and a significant reduction in maternal death. Most importantly, we would have happier mothers and healthier babies. When we pray for our women in labor, God releases supernatural strength to the mother. This strength makes the totality of the delivery process easier on the mother and child.

I can never forget the supernatural events of the delivery of Joshua, our third son. I was very weak, having been sick for ten weeks. When I fell into labor, I only had feeble contractions. This was not a good sign. The Bible says in Isaiah 37:3, that, "This is a day of trouble, and rebuke, and blasphemy; for the children have come to birth, but there is no strength to bring them forth." Our pastor and my husband prayed for me in the hospital. Afterwards, they went back home to rest. The Lord answered their prayers by fire. At midnight, an angel came to deliver me. I felt a **BIG HAND** `break the tightness around my cervix, starting off a series of very powerful contractions. Within a twinkling of an eye, the baby was out! It was like a dream! (Ps. 126:1). I am eternally grateful to God for the great deliverance He wrought in my life.

Father God, I pray that You will grace the delivery of my baby with Your presence. I ask, Oh! Lord, that Your angels will be on assignment to help me bring forth this child. Amen.

25. WOMEN OF FAITH

*Nevertheless she will be saved in childbearing
if they continue in faith, love and holiness
with self control (1 Tim. 2:15).*

This key verse is an express promise for Christian
women. It was given through the great Apostle Paul.
This statement broke the power of the generational
curse of painful childbirth on women. There are a
few conditions attached to this promise; such women
should be born again and redeemed by the blood of
Jesus Christ. They are to continue in

Faith: We need to still be in Christ, trusting
Him daily and working out our salvation with fear
and trembling. "But without faith, it is impossible to
please Him, for he who comes to God must believe
that He is, and that He is a rewarder of those who
diligently seek Him" (Heb. 11:6). Our lives have to
be pleasing in His sight.

Love: "Now hope does not disappoint, because
the love of God has been poured out in our hearts by
the Holy Spirit who was given us" (Rom. 5:5). God
wants us to put His love to work, to love Him with
all our hearts and to love our neighbor as ourselves
(Matt. 22:37-39). He wants us to be quick to forgive
and not hold grudges. Faith works by love (Gal. 5:6);
accordingly, as we walk in love, our faith will work
for us.

Holiness: "For I am the Lord your God, you shall
therefore consecrate yourselves, and you shall be

holy; for I am holy" (Lev. 11:44b). The Bible encourages us to "Pursue peace with all people and holiness, without which no man will see God" (Heb. 12:14). Although we have been made holy by His precious blood, the Lord would still have us depart from iniquity. We should not live our lives in willful sin. We need to create the atmosphere around our lives that is conducive for the Holy Spirit to dwell in.

Sobriety: Interestingly, one of the meanings of this word is abstinence from alcoholic drinks. This is the second time we see the Bible speak against drinking in women especially in relation to pregnancy. Also, sobriety means being serious minded and sober, being moderate in all things. The Apostle Paul was saying here, that, if a woman maintains these spiritual attributes in her life; she automatically becomes a candidate for safe delivery.

Dear Lord Jesus, I thank You for shedding Your blood for me that I might be redeemed from the curse of painful childbirth. Let my life please You in all things. Make me a virtuous woman indeed. Amen.

26. GENERATIONAL BLESSINGS

They shall not labor in vain, nor bring forth for trouble, for they are the seed of the blessed of the Lord, and their offspring with them (Isa. 65:23 KJV).

This is another sweet promise to us from the scriptures. To qualify for this promise, you have to be **"The seed of the Blessed."** That means you either have to be a direct descendant of Abraham through Isaac and Jacob (Israelite), or a Christian. By virtue of our faith in Christ, we are joint heirs of all the promises God gave to Abraham (Gal. 3:29).

The promise is two-fold; "You will not labor in vain." This means that all your effort in the previous nine months, culminating into the process of labor, will not be wasted. You will fall into labor and bring forth lively and healthy babies.

Secondly, "You will not bring forth for trouble."This means that your children will be well-formed, free from the generational diseases that afflicted your forebears. Your children will not bring trouble to you after they are born, they will not be prone to accidents and disasters. Rather, they will be taught of the Lord, and great shall be their peace. (Isa. 54:13).

This promise reflects how God's blessing is transferred from one generation to the next. The promise is a kind of comprehensive insurance. It covered the ancestors (Abrahamic covenant). It is now on you (the parents), and is available to your offspring. Even if you had a bad family history in the area of delivery and childbirth, once you come under the covering of the blood of Jesus Christ by faith, those curses will have to cease. You have received a new DNA in Christ; therefore your genes have to line up with the word of God. Confess this verse throughout your pregnancy. Stand on God's word with boldness. Don't back up, and don't give in. You will see the negative pattern reversed. You and your generations will be delivered. "Therefore if the Son makes you free, you shall be free indeed" (John 8:36).

Dear Lord, I thank You for extending Your saving grace to my generation, and for giving me access into Abraham's blessing by the shedding of Your blood. Let Your blessings flow to my children and grandchildren. Amen.

27. A FULL QUIVER

"Shall I bring to the time of birth, and not cause delivery?" Says the Lord. "Shall I who cause delivery shut up the womb?" Says your God" (Isa. 66:9).

This is a very specific promise, issued directly from God the Father to His beloved daughters. In this key verse, God promised that He will bring you to labor, and bring forth your baby. This is a full promise for safe and easy delivery. Furthermore, He says that even after you've had the baby, He will not shut your womb. That means that you will get pregnant again as soon as you wish.

Instances of this can be found in the lives of some women in the Bible whose wombs God opened. Rachel was barren for many years before she had Joseph. Shortly after that, she got pregnant again with Benjamin, because her womb had been opened and could no longer be shut (Rev. 3:7). Hannah is another famous example. She also used to be barren; but she was blessed with five more children after the birth of Samuel (1 Sam. 2:21). I believe the Lord wants to keep giving us children until our quivers are full, according to Psalm 127:5.

While in labor for Joshua, I said to myself "I am done with pregnancies." I had prayed for a girl, but at that point, the baby's sex became irrelevant. I just wanted to be free. I announced to all my friends that I was done having babies. I was wrong. God overlooked my shortsightedness, He insisted on answering my prayer for a daughter. He gave me double for my trouble, and later blessed us with two precious daughters. I would advise that you give no expression to any negative thought that crosses your mind in the heat of labor. If you have said any contrary words in the past, this will be a good time to erase those words by the blood of the Lamb. It is written, "The Lord shall increase you more and more; you and your children" (Ps. 115:14 KJV).

Dear Father, I thank You for Your multiple blessings in my life. Thank You for this baby in my womb, and her siblings. Amen.

28. WHAT IS ON YOUR MIND?

For thus says the Lord, "Behold, I will extend peace to her like a river, and the glory of the Gentiles like a flowing stream; then you shall feed; on her side shall you be carried, and be dandled upon her knees" (Isa. 66:12).

A pregnant woman's dreams are full of the activities she will be doing with her child once she is born. She has imaginations of nursing the baby and caring for her. This key verse illustrates a mother nurturing, cuddling and having fun with her baby. This was the picture God painted concerning Jerusalem when the nation of Israel was in exile, to encourage them that they would yet prosper as a people.

This is another of Mark's favorite scriptures. It was the promise God gave him when I developed health problems at the time I was expecting Joshua. The devil had been whispering in my husband's ears that he would lose his wife and baby. As he sought the Lord, this promise came alive for him. The Lord replaced the picture of mourning with that of a mother (me), nursing the baby (Joshua) and dandling him on my knees. We memorized this scripture. It soon became our most lethal weapon of spiritual warfare. Praise God! The word worked for us. The Lord supernaturally turned the situation in our favor. I had the baby, nursed him for eleven months, bore him on my sides, and dandled him upon my knees.

What mental images do you allow in your mind? What daydreams are you having? What about your night dreams? Entertain thoughts of happiness and good times about you and your baby. Cast down any negative image that does not line up with the mind of God concerning you (2 Cor. 10:5). Pray that the Lord will grant you His peace that passes all under-standing (Phil. 4:7). Ask God to extend to you the glory of the Gentiles like a flowing stream. Then go ahead and enjoy your baby.

Dear Father, I thank You for Your manifold good thoughts towards me. Help me Lord to transmit these thoughts unto my baby. I blot out every contrary imagination, concerning my baby and me, by the blood of Jesus. Let Your will be perfected in our lives. Amen.

29. REBUKE THE DEVOURER

And I will rebuke the devourer for your sakes, and he shall not destroy the fruits of your ground; neither shall your vine cast her fruit before time in your field (Mal. 3:11 KJV).

This is a promise given to Christians who faithfully give their tithe to God. It was an incentive to encourage the Israelites to give God a tenth of their income. In exchange for their tithes, God gave them supernatural crop protection. The same promise still holds true for us today. What has tithing got to do with delivery? A lot. This promise has deep undertones. It was originally an agricultural promise for good crop yield. A promise like this always links to the economy of the nation. However, the same principles can be applied to pregnancy and delivery. The devourer is a real enemy. He seeks to truncate your efforts, destroy the work of your hands, and, if possible, abort the fruit of your body through miscarriage. You cannot stop the devourer on your own, but God says He will rebuke the devourer for your sake.

When I fell into pre-term labor with Mercy-Grace, I panicked for fear that I might lose the baby. Right there in the emergency room, God spoke to my heart that the baby would live. The pregnancy stabilized, but my water had broken. I had to be on bed rest at the hospital waiting until she was born. It turned out to be a seven-day wait! On the sixth night God gave me this word, **"Neither shall your vine**

cast her fruit before time in your field." The baby arrived the following day; although she came ten weeks early, she did not need any kind of support; the Lord accelerated her maturation, so she behaved like a full-term baby.

Should we discuss money in a pregnancy book? Yes, we must talk about money, because tithing is intricately linked to fruitfulness. I want to believe that you faithfully give a tithe of your income to God. If not, I encourage you to start doing so now. Put God to test. He will not only bless you in return, He will see to it that you have no records of loss.

Dear Father, I thank You for supplying all my needs. As I respond by faith to pay my tithe, open the windows of heaven upon me, so that I will not have enough room to contain Your blessings. Amen.

30. JOYFUL ANTICIPATION

They that sow in tears shall reap in joy. He, who continually goes forth weeping bearing seed for sowing, shall doubtless come again with rejoicing, bringing his sheaves with him (Ps. 126:5-6).

Congratulations! It's time to rejoice and celebrate. You can hear the sounds of joy in your spirit, your baby's cry! You have carried the baby for nine months - riding the pregnancy roller-coaster. You started with nausea and morning sickness, dizziness and fatigue. You have craved strange foods, eaten all you can, only to throw it all up. You have been moody. You have cried for no reason. You have gotten tired even when doing little or no work. You have had good days. You have enjoyed loads of attention and affection from loved ones, and tender loving care from your spouse.

You are in good health. You have faithfully attended your pre-natal appointments, and you have adhered to all the doctor's rules. You have been stretched to full capacity; you have added on ten pounds and cannot find a side to sleep on. Your shoulders are thrown backwards; you walk with the pregnancy pride. Your skin is glowing, your hair is full, your breasts are engorged with milk, and your face is all puffed up! Your baby is kicking and playing within you. She sleeps all day and kicks all night. "It's tight in here, Mom, I need more space." "It's about time you came out, baby." You coo back to her.

You have prayed and meditated on the word; you have memorized and confessed scriptures. You can't wait to behold the angelic face of your infant. She is equally eager to meet you. You have done all. Now stand (Eph. 6:13). You have sown in tears. Now reap in joy. Bless the Lord in your soul and rejoice in anticipation. "Being confident of this very thing, that He who has begun a good work in you will complete it until the day of Jesus Christ" (Phil. 1:8). Amen.

Father, I thank You for seeing me to the end of this pregnancy. I rejoice in anticipation of the safe delivery of my baby. Many will rejoice with me at the birth of this child. I will stand before the congregation of Your people to declare your works. Amen.